Unlocking The Digital Frontier

A Guide to investing in Digital Assets

Davis Kemppianen

"We have elected to put our money and faith in a mathematical framework that is free of politics and human error."

Tyler Winklevoss, CEO of Gemini

Authors Notes

As a child, I was always captivated by stories of discovery—adventurers charting unknown territories, explorers unlocking the mysteries of uncharted lands, and scientists unveiling the secrets of the universe. These tales ignited in me an insatiable curiosity and a relentless desire to understand the world around me. Fast forward to adulthood, and I found myself standing at the crossroads of a new frontier—the world of digital assets. It was a landscape that seemed to evolve daily, marked by unprecedented innovations and limitless possibilities. Yet, I quickly realized that this new frontier was as bewildering as it was exciting.

My first encounter with cryptocurrencies was both thrilling and intimidating. I remember the moment vividly: a casual conversation with a friend who spoke passionately about Bitcoin, explaining its potential to revolutionize finance. At that moment, I felt a spark—a glimpse into a future where traditional financial systems could be disrupted, and ownership could be redefined. However, as the conversation deepened, I was struck by a profound sense of confusion. Terms like "blockchain," "smart contracts," and "decentralized finance" flew around the room like a foreign language I desperately wanted to understand but couldn't quite grasp.

That initial intrigue turned into a quest for knowledge. I began to seek out information, immersing myself in articles, podcasts, and online forums, trying to make sense of this rapidly changing world. But as I dug deeper, I encountered a challenge: much of the information available was either overly technical or filled with jargon that made it inaccessible for someone just starting their journey. I longed for a guide—a comprehensive resource that would bridge the gap between the complexity of digital assets and the curiosity of eager learners like me.

This desire for clarity and understanding fueled my journey. I attended meetups, engaging with seasoned investors who generously shared their experiences. I took online courses, absorbing everything I could about blockchain technology and the myriad digital assets emerging in the market. Yet, even as I acquired knowledge, I often felt overwhelmed by the sheer volume of information and the constant evolution of the landscape. Each day brought new developments, new projects, and new opportunities, but also new risks and uncertainties.

Through this journey, I realized that many others shared my struggle. Friends and family often expressed interest in digital assets but felt apprehensive about navigating the complexities. Their hesitation echoed my own initial confusion and highlighted the need for a straightforward guide that would empower individuals to explore the world of digital assets with confidence. I envisioned a resource that would demystify the concepts, clarify the intricacies, and provide practical insights for anyone looking to invest.

Thus, this book was born—not just as a collection of information, but as a compass for those embarking on their own journeys into the digital asset landscape. It is designed to be a friendly companion, guiding you step by step through the essential concepts, the promise and potential of digital assets, and the practical strategies for investing wisely. I want to share not only what I have learned but also the mistakes I made along the way and the lessons I wish I had known earlier.

As you read these pages, my hope is that you will feel inspired to explore, to ask questions, and to engage with this vibrant and dynamic community. Whether you are a complete novice or someone with a basic understanding looking to deepen your knowledge, this book aims to provide the clarity and confidence needed to navigate the digital asset world.

This journey is not just about financial investment; it is about embracing a new paradigm of ownership, value, and innovation. It is about recognizing that we are part of something larger than ourselves—an evolving ecosystem that has the power to reshape industries, redefine wealth, and democratize access to financial opportunities. As we venture together through the chapters ahead, I encourage you to approach this journey with an open mind and a willingness to learn.

Welcome to the world of digital assets—a world brimming with promise, possibility, and potential. Together, let's unlock the doors to this exciting new realm and empower ourselves to become informed and engaged investors in this digital revolution. Your journey begins here.

Chapter 1:
What is a Digital Asset?

In a world where much of our daily lives exist online, the concept of assets is evolving. What was once limited to physical items like cash, real estate, and gold, or more abstract financial tools like stocks and bonds, has expanded to include *digital assets*. Understanding digital assets is foundational to navigating the modern economy, especially as more value moves onto the internet and the blockchain. But what exactly is a digital asset, and how does it differ from traditional assets?

Defining Digital Assets

At its simplest, a digital asset is anything that exists in a digital format and comes with rights of use or ownership. However, the significance of digital assets goes far beyond a simple PDF document, music file, or image saved on your computer. Digital assets today represent a broad and rapidly growing category of investments, ownership, and utility—driven by the power of blockchain technology.

Digital assets can include cryptocurrencies, tokens, non-fungible tokens (NFTs), smart contracts, decentralized applications (dApps), and more. Each of these operates in a digital space but carries different properties in terms of ownership, utility, and transferability.

Let's break down the types of digital assets to understand them better.

Types of Digital Assets:

- Cryptocurrencies
- Tokens
- Non-Fungible Tokens
- Stable Coins
- Decentralized digital assets (Defi)

Cryptocurrencies:

Cryptocurrencies are the most well-known type of digital asset, often used interchangeably with the term itself. Bitcoin, the first cryptocurrency, was introduced in 2009 by an anonymous person (or group) known as Satoshi Nakamoto. It was designed as a decentralized currency, operating outside the control of any central authority or government.

Bitcoin isn't the only cryptocurrency, though. Thousands of others have since emerged, each with different purposes, designs, and applications. Ethereum, for instance, is both a cryptocurrency and a platform for building decentralized applications. Litecoin, Cardano, Solana, and many others are part of this rapidly growing ecosystem.

Tokens:

In the world of blockchain, the term "token" is often used to describe digital assets that represent something other than currency. These tokens can be built on existing blockchains, such as Ethereum, where they follow a specific set of standards (such as ERC-20 tokens).

Tokens generally fall into three categories:

- *Utility Tokens:* These provide access to a product or service, much like a voucher or coupon. They do not necessarily represent ownership in a company but rather offer functionality within a particular project. For example, "Filecoin" is a utility token used to access decentralized storage services.
- *Security Tokens*: Security tokens represent ownership in a real-world asset, such as equity in a company or a piece of real estate. They are regulated more like traditional financial securities

and offer investors certain rights, such as dividends or voting power.
- *Governance Tokens*: These tokens grant holders the right to vote on decisions in a decentralized network or project. "Uniswap (UNI)" is an example, where token holders vote on changes to the platform.

Non-Fungible Tokens (NFTs):

One of the most talked-about developments in the digital asset world in recent years is the rise of Non-Fungible Tokens, or NFTs. While cryptocurrencies like Bitcoin and Ethereum are fungible (one Bitcoin is equivalent to any other Bitcoin), NFTs are unique and represent ownership of a specific digital item or piece of content.

NFTs can represent digital art, music, videos, virtual real estate, in-game assets, or even tweets. The ownership of these digital items is verified on a blockchain, meaning that anyone can verify who owns the original, even if the content itself can be copied. This uniqueness gives NFTs their value, particularly in digital art markets where collectors may pay millions for a one-of-a-kind piece of digital art.

However, NFTs go beyond art. They are used in a range of industries, including:

Gaming: Players can own, trade, or sell virtual goods or characters, which are represented as NFTs.

Virtual Real Estate: Platforms like **Decentraland** allow users to buy virtual land or property, which exists entirely in a digital world.

Collectibles: Similar to physical trading cards, digital collectibles like NBA Top Shot moments have become highly valuable.

Stablecoins:

While the prices of cryptocurrencies like Bitcoin and Ethereum fluctuate wildly, stablecoins aim to offer price stability. These digital assets are typically pegged to the value of a stable asset, like the US dollar or gold.

For example, Tether (USDT and USD Coin (USDC) or Ripple USD (RLUSD) are stablecoins that maintain a 1:1 value with the US dollar. Stablecoins serve as a bridge between traditional finance and the cryptocurrency world, offering the benefits of digital assets (such as easy transferability and decentralized control) without the volatility of other cryptocurrencies.

Decentralized Finance (DeFi) Assets:

Decentralized finance, or "DeFi" refers to the ecosystem of financial products and services built on blockchain networks. DeFi allows users to lend, borrow, trade, and earn interest on their digital assets without relying on traditional intermediaries like banks or brokers.

DeFi assets include tokens that represent liquidity in decentralized exchanges, loans, or other financial products. These assets operate in decentralized applications (dApps) that use smart contracts to execute transactions automatically based on predefined rules.

DeFi represents a radical departure from traditional financial systems, offering opportunities for investors to earn yields and participate in financial services in a completely decentralized manner.

Chapter 2:
Cryptocurrencies have three core characteristics

Cryptocurrencies are more than just a digital alternative to traditional money; they represent a radical rethinking of the concept of currency and how it works in the modern world. At their foundation, cryptocurrencies share three core characteristics that set them apart from traditional financial systems: **decentralization, cryptographic security, and transparency**. These principles are not just technical features—they are the cornerstones that make cryptocurrencies unique, offering new possibilities for financial inclusion, innovation, and security.

In this chapter, we will dive into each of these core characteristics to understand how they define the world of cryptocurrencies, and how they are transforming our understanding of money and ownership in a digital era.

Decentralization: The Power of No Central Authority:

Perhaps the most revolutionary aspect of cryptocurrencies is their decentralized nature. Unlike traditional currencies, which are issued and controlled by central banks or governments, cryptocurrencies are not managed by any single institution. Instead, they operate on a decentralized network of computers (known as **nodes**) that work together to verify and record transactions on a public ledger called the **blockchain**.

How Decentralization Works

In traditional financial systems, banks and central authorities are responsible for verifying transactions and maintaining ledgers of who owns what. If you make a payment using a credit card or bank transfer, for instance, a centralized institution verifies the transaction and adjusts its records accordingly. This means that we place a lot of trust in these intermediaries to process transactions fairly, securely, and transparently.

Cryptocurrencies remove this need for a trusted intermediary. In a decentralized cryptocurrency network, all participating nodes have a copy of the blockchain, which is constantly updated with new transactions. Transactions are verified through a process known as **consensus**, meaning that the majority of nodes in the network must agree that the transaction is valid before it is added to the blockchain.

This decentralization offers several key benefits:

- *Resilience*: Because there is no central point of failure, decentralized networks are more resilient to attacks or disruptions. If one node or even a group of nodes fails, the rest of the network can continue to function.

- *Reduced Censorship*: In a decentralized system, no single entity has the power to censor or block transactions. This gives users greater freedom to transfer funds without interference from governments or corporations.
- *Empowerment of Users*: With cryptocurrencies, individuals have full control over their funds, without needing to rely on banks or third parties to manage their wealth. This is particularly powerful in regions where access to banking services is limited.

The Challenge of Decentralization

However, decentralization also comes with challenges. One key issue is scalability—decentralized systems can be slower and less efficient than centralized systems because they require multiple nodes to verify each transaction. This is one reason why cryptocurrency transactions can sometimes take longer to process, especially during times of high network traffic.

Furthermore, while decentralization provides more control to individual users, it also means that users bear the full responsibility for managing their digital assets. If you lose access to your cryptocurrency wallet's private keys, for instance, there is no central authority to help you recover your funds. This is why understanding and securely managing cryptocurrency wallets is essential for any user.

Cryptographic Security: Protecting Transactions and Ownership:

The second defining characteristic of cryptocurrencies is **cryptographic security**. Cryptocurrencies leverage advanced cryptography to secure transactions, control the creation of new units, and ensure the integrity of the blockchain. This is one of the key reasons why blockchain technology is often described as **tamper-resistant**.

The Role of Cryptography in Cryptocurrencies

Cryptography is the practice of securing information through mathematical algorithms. In the context of cryptocurrencies, two main cryptographic techniques are used: public-key cryptography and hashing.

- *Public-Key Cryptography*: In cryptocurrencies, every user has a pair of cryptographic keys: a public key and a private key. The public key is like an address that can be shared with others to receive funds. The private key, however, is kept secret and is used to sign transactions. This cryptographic signature is what allows users to prove ownership of their funds and authorize transfers.
  For example, if Alice wants to send 1 Bitcoin to Bob, she uses her private key to sign the

transaction. This signature is verified by nodes in the network using Alice's public key, ensuring that she is the rightful owner of the Bitcoin she is sending and that the transaction hasn't been altered in any way.
- *Hashing*: Hashing is another cryptographic process used to secure data on the blockchain. A hash function takes input data (such as a block of transactions) and produces a fixed-length string of characters. This string is unique to the input data, meaning that even a small change in the input will result in a completely different hash. Hashing ensures the integrity of the blockchain, as each block in the chain contains the hash of the previous block, making it extremely difficult to alter past transactions without being detected.

Security Through Consensus

Cryptocurrencies also rely on cryptographic consensus mechanisms to verify transactions. The most well-known of these mechanisms is Proof of Work (PoW), used by Bitcoin. In PoW, nodes (known as miners) compete to solve complex mathematical problems in order to add a new block of transactions to the blockchain. The first miner to solve the problem broadcasts the solution to the network, and if the majority of nodes agree that the solution is correct, the new block is added to the chain.

Other cryptocurrencies use different consensus mechanisms, such as Proof of Stake (PoS), which selects validators based on the amount of cryptocurrency they hold. These mechanisms ensure that transactions are verified in a secure and decentralized manner.

The Benefits of Cryptographic Security

The use of cryptography in cryptocurrencies offers several significant advantages:

- *Tamper Resistance*: Once a transaction is recorded on the blockchain, it cannot be altered or deleted without the agreement of the entire network. This makes cryptocurrency systems highly resistant to fraud and tampering.
- *Anonymity and Privacy*: While public blockchains are transparent (as we'll explore in the next section), they also offer a degree of privacy. Users can conduct transactions without revealing their personal identity, as transactions are associated with cryptographic addresses rather than real-world names.
- *Global Security*: Cryptocurrencies operate on a global scale, and cryptography ensures that transactions are secure no matter where they take place. Whether you're sending Bitcoin from New York to Tokyo or using it to buy a coffee, the underlying cryptography guarantees the integrity of the transaction.

Transparency: A New Era of Financial Openness:

The third core characteristic of cryptocurrencies is **transparency**. Most cryptocurrencies operate on public blockchains, where every transaction is visible to anyone who wants to view it. This level of transparency is unprecedented in the world of finance and offers a new level of openness that has both benefits and challenges.

How Transparency Works in Cryptocurrencies

In a public blockchain, every transaction is recorded in an open ledger. This means that anyone, anywhere in the world, can view the full transaction history of a given cryptocurrency. While the identities of users are not revealed (only their cryptographic addresses are), the transparency of the system allows for full verification of the blockchain's accuracy.

This level of openness stands in stark contrast to traditional financial systems, where transactions are often private, opaque, and subject to oversight by centralized institutions. For example, if you send money via a bank transfer, only you, the bank, and the recipient are privy to the details of the transaction. In cryptocurrency networks, on the other hand, all participants have access to the blockchain's full history.

The Benefits of Transparency

Transparency in cryptocurrencies provides several key advantages:

- *Auditability*: Because all transactions are public, cryptocurrencies can be easily audited by anyone. This makes it more difficult for bad actors to engage in fraudulent behavior, as all activities are recorded in an immutable ledger.
- *Trustless Transactions*: Cryptocurrencies allow for **trustless** transactions, meaning that two parties can transact without needing to trust each other or a central intermediary. The blockchain itself acts as the source of truth, providing all the information needed to verify the legitimacy of a transaction.
- *Reduced Corruption*: In traditional financial systems, corruption and fraud can be difficult to detect due to the opacity of transactions. The transparency of cryptocurrencies makes it harder for individuals or institutions to manipulate financial records without being caught.

The Challenges of Transparency

While transparency is a powerful feature, it also raises privacy concerns. Even though users' real identities are not linked to their cryptocurrency addresses, sophisticated methods can sometimes be used to deanonymize transactions. As a result, privacy-focused cryptocurrencies like Monero and Zcash have emerged to offer more anonymity by obfuscating transaction details.

Furthermore, the public nature of blockchain transactions can create challenges for businesses or individuals who need to protect sensitive financial information. As cryptocurrency adoption grows, striking a balance between transparency and privacy will be an ongoing challenge for the industry.

The three core characteristics of cryptocurrencies—decentralization, cryptographic security, and transparency—are the foundation of what makes these digital assets revolutionary. They not only redefine how we think about money but also how we engage with financial systems, security, and trust. By eliminating the need for intermediaries, providing security through cryptography, and fostering transparency, cryptocurrencies offer a new paradigm for global finance.

Chapter 3:
How Digital Assets Differ from Traditional Assets

The rapid growth of digital assets has forced investors, regulators, and businesses to rethink long-established ideas about ownership, value, and finance. While traditional assets—like stocks, bonds, real estate, and commodities—are deeply rooted in the physical world or centralized financial systems, digital assets exist in a decentralized, digital space, often governed by blockchain technology. Understanding the key differences between these two categories is crucial for navigating the new digital economy.

In this chapter, we will explore how digital assets differ from traditional assets across various dimensions: ownership, transferability, liquidity, regulation, and accessibility. These differences highlight the revolutionary potential of digital assets and the new opportunities and challenges they present.

Ownership: From Custodianship to Self-Sovereignty

One of the fundamental differences between traditional and digital assets is how ownership is managed. Traditional assets rely heavily on trusted intermediaries and centralized systems to maintain records of ownership, while digital assets place ownership directly in the hands of the individual.

Traditional Assets

In traditional financial systems, ownership is usually custodial. This means third-party institutions, such as banks, brokers, or government agencies, hold and manage assets on behalf of the owner. For example:

- *Stocks* are held in brokerage accounts, with centralized clearinghouses like the Depository Trust & Clearing Corporation (DTCC) ensuring the ownership is properly recorded.
- *Real estate:* ownership is documented in public registries maintained by local or national governments, requiring a legal process to transfer ownership.
- *Bank accounts*: deposits are held in banks, with the bank acting as the custodian of the funds.

In these systems, asset holders depend on intermediaries to verify, maintain, and safeguard their ownership. While this provides convenience and legal protections, it also means that individuals don't have direct control over their assets.

Digital Assets

Digital assets flip this traditional model by enabling self-sovereign ownership through cryptographic keys.

Instead of relying on third-party institutions to verify ownership, digital assets like cryptocurrencies are controlled directly by the owner:

- *Private keys*: used to prove ownership and control over digital assets. Whoever holds the private key associated with a digital asset has full control over it, with no need for intermediaries like banks or brokers.
- *Blockchain*: ensures that ownership records are decentralized and immutable. Transactions are validated and recorded by a distributed network of computers, making it virtually impossible to alter ownership records without consensus from the network.

This direct form of ownership is empowering, but it comes with significant responsibility. If an individual loses their private key, they lose access to their digital assets, and there is no central authority that can restore ownership. This level of self-custody is a double-edged sword, offering autonomy but requiring enhanced security practices.

Transferability: Instant, Borderless Transactions

The ability to transfer assets is another key area where digital assets differ from traditional ones. Traditional asset transfers are often slow, costly, and dependent on intermediaries, whereas digital assets can be transferred quickly and efficiently across borders, often without intermediaries.

Traditional Assets

Transferring traditional assets usually involves multiple parties and can be time-consuming:

- Bank transfers between accounts, particularly international ones, can take days and involve high fees due to the need for currency exchange, compliance checks, and intermediary banks.
- Stock trades require clearinghouses and brokerage platforms, and settlement periods can take days.
- Real estate transfers involve legal processes, title checks, and government registrations, which can take weeks or even months to complete.

These systems are highly regulated to ensure the legitimacy of transfers, but they also introduce delays and costs.

Digital Assets

Digital assets, especially cryptocurrencies, are designed for fast, efficient, and borderless transfers:

- Cryptocurrency transactions can be completed within minutes, regardless of geographic location. Whether sending Bitcoin from one wallet to another or transferring Ethereum across a decentralized exchange, the process is typically much faster than traditional asset transfers.
- Peer-to-peer transfers are a defining feature of digital assets. Without needing intermediaries like banks or brokers, digital assets can be transferred directly between individuals or entities, reducing costs and speeding up the process.

This ability to transfer value quickly and globally has profound implications, particularly for international remittances, cross-border trade, and financial inclusion in underbanked regions.

Decentralization vs. Centralization: Rethinking Trust

Another major distinction between digital and traditional assets lies in how they are managed and governed. Traditional financial systems are centralized, relying on trusted institutions to oversee asset management. Digital assets, on the other hand, often operate in decentralized networks where trust is placed in the code and consensus mechanisms, rather than institutions.

Traditional Assets

In traditional finance, centralization is key to ensuring the integrity of the system:

- Banks are trusted to manage deposits, facilitate transfers, and provide credit.
- Stock exchanges operate under the oversight of regulators like the Securities and Exchange Commission (SEC), ensuring that trades are fair, transparent, and legal.
- Governments maintain real estate registries and enforce property laws to verify ownership and transfers.

Centralized systems provide a sense of stability and legal recourse, but they also create single points of failure. For instance, if a bank is compromised or a central authority is corrupt, the system can collapse or become inefficient.

Digital Assets

Digital assets, particularly those built on blockchain, leverage decentralization to create trust:

- Cryptocurrencies like Bitcoin and Ethereum operate on decentralized networks where no single entity has control. Instead, transactions are verified

by a global network of nodes that follow strict consensus protocols.
- Smart contracts on blockchain networks allow for the automatic execution of agreements without the need for intermediaries, providing transparency and reducing the risk of fraud.

This decentralization reduces reliance on centralized institutions and allows for more resilient, censorship-resistant financial systems. However, it also introduces challenges around governance, security, and regulatory compliance, which are still evolving.

Liquidity: Flexibility and 24/7 Markets

Liquidity, or the ease with which an asset can be converted into cash or other assets, is another area where digital and traditional assets diverge. Traditional assets often have limited liquidity and are constrained by market hours, while digital assets offer greater flexibility and around-the-clock trading.

Traditional Assets

Traditional asset markets are often constrained by time and process:
- Stock markets have specific trading hours, and trades are subject to regulatory scrutiny and settlement periods.

- Real estate is highly illiquid, as properties can take months or even years to sell, with high transaction costs and long closing processes.
- Commodities like gold and oil also have limited liquidity, with trades confined to certain exchanges and timeframes.

These systems are well-established and offer stability, but they also limit investors' ability to quickly convert assets into cash or make trades outside of market hours.

Digital Assets

Digital assets, by contrast, offer much greater liquidity and flexibility:

- Cryptocurrencies are traded on a variety of global exchanges, many of which operate 24/7. This means investors can buy, sell, or trade assets at any time, regardless of traditional market hours.
- Decentralized exchanges (DEXs) allow users to trade digital assets without relying on centralized intermediaries, providing even more liquidity and accessibility.
- Tokenized assets can represent fractions of real-world assets like real estate or art, making traditionally illiquid investments more accessible and tradable.

This continuous, global marketplace offers investors more flexibility, though it can also lead to increased volatility, especially in emerging digital asset markets.

Regulation: Navigating Uncharted Territory

Traditional assets operate within well-established regulatory frameworks that provide legal protections and ensure market stability. Digital assets, on the other hand, are still navigating a complex and evolving regulatory environment, with rules varying widely by jurisdiction.

Traditional Assets

Traditional financial assets are heavily regulated to protect investors and ensure the integrity of markets:

- Stock markets are overseen by regulatory bodies like the SEC, which enforce transparency, insider trading laws, and investor protections.
- Banking is subject to stringent capital requirements, anti-money laundering (AML) regulations, and consumer protection laws.
- Real estate transactions must comply with local property laws, zoning regulations, and tax requirements.

These regulations create a stable environment for investors, but they also limit flexibility and innovation, as compliance can be costly and time-consuming.

Digital Assets

The regulatory landscape for digital assets is still in flux, with different countries and regions taking varied approaches:

- Cryptocurrencies are often seen as decentralized, borderless assets, but they are subject to increasing scrutiny from regulators concerned with fraud, tax evasion, and market manipulation.
- Initial coin offerings (ICOs), DeFi platforms, and NFTs have faced varying levels of regulation, with some jurisdictions banning or heavily regulating these activities while others embrace them as innovative financial instruments.
- Central Bank Digital Currencies (CBDCs) represent a new frontier, as governments explore digital versions of national currencies, blending traditional regulatory oversight with the flexibility of digital assets.

The evolving nature of digital asset regulation creates uncertainty, but it also offers opportunities for innovation and reform in global financial systems.

Digital assets represent a fundamental shift from the traditional ways in which we understand and interact with value. Unlike traditional assets, which are tied to physical systems, intermediaries, and centralized authorities, digital assets offer a more decentralized, autonomous, and flexible approach to ownership, transferability, and market participation.

While the promise of digital assets is enormous—offering greater liquidity, faster transactions, and more inclusive financial opportunities—these innovations also come with new risks and challenges. Security, regulation, and the need for personal responsibility in managing digital assets are all critical considerations as this space continues to evolve.

Understanding the key differences between digital and traditional assets is essential for investors, businesses, and policymakers looking to navigate the rapidly changing landscape of the digital economy.

Chapter 4:
The Promise and Potential of Digital Assets

Digital assets have rapidly transformed from niche curiosities into a major force in the financial world, signaling a shift in how value is created, transferred, and stored. The promise of digital assets extends far beyond cryptocurrencies like Bitcoin and Ethereum. These innovations hold the potential to revolutionize industries, reshape traditional financial systems, and offer new opportunities for investment, economic inclusion, and decentralization.

In this chapter, we will explore the promise and potential of digital assets across various domains, from reshaping financial systems to driving innovation and empowering individuals. We'll delve into how they are transforming ownership, investing, and the global economy.

Democratizing Access to Financial Services

One of the most significant promises of digital assets is their ability to democratize access to financial services, especially for those who are unbanked or underbanked. Traditional financial systems rely heavily on intermediaries like banks, which can be inaccessible to many due to geographical, economic, or political reasons.

A New Path for the Unbanked

According to the World Bank, over 1.4 billion people globally lack access to basic banking services. Digital assets, particularly cryptocurrencies, can provide these individuals with an alternative way to store, transfer, and access value, without needing a traditional bank account:

- Cryptocurrencies enable anyone with an internet connection to send and receive payments across borders at a fraction of the cost charged by traditional remittance services.
- Decentralized Finance (DeFi) offers services like borrowing, lending, and saving without intermediaries, making financial products more accessible to a broader population. Platforms like Compound and Aave allow users to earn interest on their assets or borrow funds without needing approval from a centralized bank or financial institution.

By removing the barriers imposed by traditional financial institutions, digital assets can promote greater financial inclusion, giving people in developing economies access to capital, investment opportunities, and new forms of financial independence.

Fractional Ownership and New Investment Opportunities

The tokenization of assets has opened up possibilities for **fractional ownership**—the ability to divide ownership of an asset into smaller, tradable pieces. This innovation is creating new opportunities for investors and transforming industries from real estate to art and collectibles.

Tokenization of Real-World Assets

Through the tokenization of physical assets, digital assets can represent ownership stakes in real estate, commodities, or even art. Tokenization allows large, expensive assets to be divided into smaller pieces, enabling fractional ownership:

- Real estate tokenization makes it possible for investors to buy shares in properties without needing to purchase the entire property. This allows small-scale investors to access the real estate market with lower capital requirements.
- Art tokenization is changing how people invest in high-value artwork. For example, platforms like Masterworks enable investors to purchase fractional shares of iconic paintings, democratizing access to art investments traditionally available only to the wealthy.

This fractional ownership model lowers the barriers to entry for investment and provides increased liquidity for traditionally illiquid markets, giving more people access to a wider range of investment opportunities.

Decentralized Finance (DeFi): Rewriting the Financial System

Decentralized Finance, or **DeFi**, is one of the most promising areas of digital asset innovation. DeFi platforms use blockchain technology to offer financial services without traditional intermediaries like banks, exchanges, or insurance companies. By leveraging smart contracts and decentralized networks, DeFi is democratizing financial services and unlocking new ways to invest, borrow, lend, and trade.

Benefits of DeFi

DeFi is transforming the financial landscape in several ways:

- Eliminating intermediaries: In traditional finance, services like borrowing, lending, and trading require intermediaries such as banks, brokers, and exchanges. DeFi platforms replace these intermediaries with smart contracts, reducing costs and increasing efficiency.
- Access to global markets: DeFi platforms are open to anyone with an internet connection, regardless of their location or background. This global accessibility provides opportunities for users in

developing economies to participate in financial markets that were previously out of reach.
- Yield farming and staking: DeFi has introduced new investment opportunities, such as yield farming and staking. Yield farming allows investors to earn interest by providing liquidity to decentralized exchanges, while staking enables users to earn rewards by participating in the network's consensus mechanisms.

DeFi is still in its early stages, but its potential to disrupt traditional financial systems and create a more open, inclusive, and transparent global financial system is immense.

Transparency, Security, and Trust

One of the key promises of digital assets lies in their ability to provide transparency and security through blockchain technology. The decentralized nature of blockchain creates trust through transparency, as every transaction is recorded on a public ledger that can be audited and verified by anyone.

Increased Transparency

Traditional financial systems often operate behind closed doors, where only regulators or authorized parties can access transaction records. In contrast, blockchain technology makes financial transactions visible to all participants, providing unparalleled transparency. For example:

- Public blockchains like Bitcoin and Ethereum allow users to view every transaction ever made, creating a trustless system where transparency is built into the protocol.
- Supply chain transparency: Blockchain is being used to improve transparency in supply chains by enabling companies and consumers to track the origins and movements of products. This can be particularly valuable in industries like food, pharmaceuticals, and fashion, where trust and authenticity are crucial.

This increased transparency reduces the likelihood of fraud and corruption, as all transactions are recorded and cannot be altered without consensus from the network.

Enhanced Security

Digital assets, especially those secured by blockchain technology, offer enhanced security features compared to traditional systems:

- Cryptographic security: Blockchain transactions are secured by cryptography, making them highly resistant to hacking and fraud.
- Immutability: Once a transaction is recorded on a blockchain, it is nearly impossible to alter or

reverse. This immutability ensures the integrity of the transaction history and prevents tampering.
- Decentralized control: Because blockchain networks are decentralized, they are less vulnerable to centralized points of failure, such as a bank or clearinghouse being hacked or compromised.

While the technology is not without its risks (such as vulnerabilities in smart contracts or security breaches in digital wallets), the overall security of blockchain-based systems represents a significant improvement over many traditional financial systems.

Non-Fungible Tokens (NFTs) and the Digital Economy

Non-fungible tokens (NFTs) represent a unique form of digital asset that has captured the public's imagination. Unlike cryptocurrencies, which are fungible (one Bitcoin is equal to another Bitcoin), NFTs are unique digital assets that represent ownership of a specific item or piece of content, such as digital art, music, or virtual real estate.

The Rise of Digital Ownership

NFTs are transforming industries like art, gaming, and entertainment by providing a new way to own, trade, and monetize digital content:

- *Digital art*: Artists can now sell their work as NFTs, allowing them to reach a global audience and retain ownership of their digital creations. Notable examples include Beeple's "Everydays: The First 5000 Days," which sold for $69 million at auction.
- *Gaming*: In the world of gaming, NFTs are being used to represent in-game assets such as weapons, characters, and skins. These assets can be owned by players and traded on secondary markets, creating new economies within virtual worlds.
- *Virtual real estate*: Platforms like Decentraland and The Sandbox allow users to buy, sell, and develop virtual land as NFTs. These virtual worlds offer new opportunities for social interaction, commerce, and entertainment, blending the lines between the physical and digital economies.

The potential of NFTs extends beyond art and gaming, with possibilities for tokenizing intellectual property, sports memorabilia, and even real-world assets. By enabling unique digital ownership, NFTs are unlocking new forms of value and transforming the way we interact with digital content.

Programmable Money and Smart Contracts

Another groundbreaking innovation in the digital asset space is the concept of programmable money and smart contracts. Unlike traditional money, which serves only as a medium of exchange, programmable money can be embedded with rules and conditions that automatically execute when certain criteria are met.

How Smart Contracts Work

Smart contracts are self-executing contracts with the terms of the agreement directly written into code. They automatically execute transactions or actions when predefined conditions are met, without the need for intermediaries:

- *Automation*: For example, a smart contract could automatically transfer payment to a supplier once a shipment of goods is confirmed to have arrived.
- *Trustless execution*: Since smart contracts run on decentralized networks like Ethereum, they don't require trust in a third party. The contract executes based on the conditions encoded into the blockchain, ensuring fairness and transparency.

The Future of Finance and Commerce

Smart contracts are poised to revolutionize industries by enabling more efficient, automated transactions. They can be applied in areas such as:

- *Insurance*: Claims can be automatically paid out when certain conditions are met, reducing paperwork and delays.

- *Real estate*: Property transfers can be automated through smart contracts, eliminating the need for costly intermediaries like notaries and lawyers.
- *Supply chains*: Payments and deliveries can be automated, creating a more seamless and transparent flow of goods and capital.

As the technology behind smart contracts continues to evolve, the potential for automated, trustless systems in finance, law, and commerce is enormous.

The Future of Work and Digital Identity

In addition to transforming financial systems, digital assets hold the potential to redefine how we work and manage digital identity. Decentralized platforms and blockchain-based identity solutions are reshaping traditional employment models and providing new ways to manage personal data.

The Decentralized Gig Economy

The rise of decentralized platforms has enabled a new kind of gig economy, where individuals can offer their services directly to others without intermediaries:

- Freelance marketplaces like Gitcoin and Braintrust allow workers to connect with employers on a peer-to-peer basis, with payments facilitated by smart contracts and cryptocurrencies.

- Token-based incentives allow workers to earn rewards for their contributions to decentralized platforms, creating new forms of employment and income generation.

Digital Identity and Self-Sovereignty

Blockchain-based identity solutions promise to give individuals greater control over their personal data:

- Self-sovereign identity systems allow individuals to own and manage their digital identities, rather than relying on centralized authorities like governments or corporations.
- Digital credentials can be stored and verified on the blockchain, enabling secure, privacy-preserving ways to share identity information.

By decentralizing identity and enabling individuals to control their data, these innovations have the potential to empower people in ways that traditional systems cannot.

The promise and potential of digital assets extend far beyond the hype of cryptocurrencies. They represent a fundamental shift in how we think about value, ownership, and finance. From democratizing access to financial services and creating new investment opportunities to transforming industries with smart contracts and tokenization, digital assets are at the forefront of a global economic revolution.

As the technology and regulatory frameworks around digital assets continue to evolve, their full potential will likely unfold, bringing about new innovations, opportunities, and challenges. The future of digital assets is filled with promise, offering a glimpse into a more decentralized, inclusive, and efficient global economy.

Chapter 5:
The Evolution of Digital Assets

The story of digital assets is one of rapid transformation, technological breakthroughs, and shifting paradigms in finance, ownership, and value creation. What began as an experiment in cryptography and decentralized currencies has evolved into a broad spectrum of asset types that touch nearly every aspect of the global economy.

In this chapter, we will explore the key phases in the evolution of digital assets, from the early days of cryptocurrencies to the emergence of decentralized finance (DeFi), tokenization of real-world assets, and the rise of non-fungible tokens (NFTs). Understanding this evolution helps contextualize the current landscape and reveals where the future of digital assets may be headed.

The Birth of Cryptocurrencies: Bitcoin and Beyond

The launch of **Bitcoin** in 2009 marked the birth of digital assets as we know them. Conceived by an individual or group under the pseudonym **Satoshi Nakamoto**, Bitcoin was designed to be a peer-to-peer electronic cash system that operated outside of traditional financial institutions. Its revolutionary ideas—decentralization, trustless transactions, and cryptographic security—set the stage for the digital asset movement.

Bitcoin: The Pioneer of Digital Assets

Bitcoin's creation was driven by dissatisfaction with the existing financial system, particularly in the wake of the 2008 global financial crisis. Traditional currencies were controlled by central banks, susceptible to inflation, and dependent on third-party institutions like banks for transactions. Bitcoin, by contrast, was built on blockchain technology, a decentralized ledger that recorded transactions across a distributed network of computers (nodes):

- *Trustless system*: Bitcoin enabled transactions to occur without intermediaries like banks or payment processors. Instead, network participants verified transactions, making the system trustless and decentralized.
- *Fixed supply*: Bitcoin's supply was capped at 21 million coins, making it a deflationary asset designed to preserve value over time.
- *Cryptographic security*: Transactions were secured through cryptography, ensuring that assets couldn't be forged or double-spent.

Bitcoin's success spawned thousands of other cryptocurrencies, each offering variations on the original concept. However, it wasn't until the creation of

Ethereum in 2015 that digital assets expanded beyond being purely currencies.

Ethereum: Smart Contracts and Programmable Money

While Bitcoin's blockchain was focused on enabling peer-to-peer transactions, Ethereum, created by Vitalik Buterin, introduced the concept of smart contracts—self-executing contracts with the terms of the agreement directly written into code. This was a game-changer:

- Smart contracts allowed developers to create decentralized applications (dApps) that could execute code automatically when certain conditions were met, without the need for a third-party intermediary.
- Decentralized finance (DeFi): Ethereum's programmable blockchain laid the groundwork for DeFi, a movement aimed at recreating traditional financial services—like lending, borrowing, and trading—on decentralized platforms.

The Rise of Decentralized Finance (DeFi)

Decentralized finance (DeFi) represents one of the most transformative phases in the evolution of digital assets. Built primarily on the Ethereum blockchain, DeFi leverages smart contracts to replicate traditional financial services without intermediaries like banks or brokers. This phase of evolution saw the rise of decentralized exchanges (DEXs), lending protocols, yield farming, and new forms of liquidity.

Key Innovations in DeFi

DeFi projects aim to create a more open, transparent, and accessible financial system. Key innovations include:

- *Decentralized exchanges (DEXs)*: Platforms like Uniswap and SushiSwap allow users to trade digital assets directly with one another, without the need for a centralized exchange or intermediary. Trades are facilitated by liquidity pools, where users provide assets in exchange for fees.
- *Yield farming and staking*: DeFi introduced new ways for users to earn passive income through their digital assets. Yield farming involves providing liquidity to DeFi protocols in exchange for rewards, while staking allows users to lock up their assets to help secure a network in return for interest.
- *Lending and borrowing*: Platforms like Compound and Aave allow users to lend out their digital assets

and earn interest, or borrow assets without needing to go through traditional banks.

DeFi projects are governed by decentralized protocols, meaning that the rules of the system are encoded into smart contracts and operate automatically. This innovation allows financial services to be more efficient, inclusive, and resistant to censorship, though it also introduces risks related to security and regulatory oversight.

The Promise and Challenges of DeFi

DeFi offers immense promise by lowering barriers to entry for financial services, providing high returns on digital assets, and fostering innovation in financial products. However, it also faces challenges:

- *Security vulnerabilities*: As smart contracts are immutable, any errors or bugs can be exploited, resulting in significant losses for users.
- *Regulatory uncertainty*: DeFi operates in a legal grey area, as many jurisdictions have yet to establish clear guidelines for decentralized finance platforms.

Despite these challenges, DeFi continues to grow rapidly, with billions of dollars locked in DeFi protocols and new projects launching regularly, pushing the boundaries of what's possible in the financial world.

Tokenization: Bridging the Physical and Digital Worlds

As the digital asset space matured, innovators began exploring how blockchain technology could be used to represent ownership of real-world assets in digital form. This process, known as **tokenization**, opened up a new frontier for digital assets, allowing physical items like real estate, commodities, and even art to be represented as tokens on a blockchain.

What is Tokenization?

Tokenization involves creating a digital representation (token) of a real-world asset on a blockchain. These tokens can then be bought, sold, or traded just like cryptocurrencies. Tokenization has the potential to democratize access to traditionally illiquid or high-value assets by allowing fractional ownership:

- *Real estate*: Investors can purchase tokens that represent a share in a property, allowing them to invest in real estate without needing to buy an entire building.
- *Commodities*: Precious metals like gold can be tokenized, allowing investors to own fractions of a gold bar and trade them on digital platforms.

- *Art and collectibles*: High-value artwork and rare collectibles can be tokenized, providing liquidity in markets that are traditionally difficult to access.

Tokenization enhances liquidity, reduces the cost of ownership, and provides broader access to assets that were previously out of reach for many investors.

The Emergence of NFTs: Ownership in the Digital Era

Perhaps the most groundbreaking development in recent years has been the rise of **non-fungible tokens (NFTs)**. While cryptocurrencies like Bitcoin and Ethereum are fungible (each unit is identical and interchangeable), NFTs represent unique digital assets. This uniqueness has unlocked new possibilities for digital ownership, particularly in the realms of art, music, and virtual goods.

What Makes NFTs Unique?

NFTs are digital assets that are indivisible, unique, and cannot be exchanged on a one-to-one basis like cryptocurrencies. Each NFT is distinct and has its own value, which is recorded on a blockchain. They are used to represent ownership of digital or physical items such as:

- *Digital art*: NFTs have become a popular way to buy, sell, and own digital artwork, with some pieces selling for millions of dollars. Artists now have a way to monetize their work directly and gain royalties each time the piece is resold.
- *Music and entertainment*: Musicians and creators use NFTs to release exclusive content, giving fans the ability to own rare or limited-edition digital goods.
- *Virtual real estate and goods*: In virtual worlds like Decentraland and The Sandbox, NFTs represent ownership of land, buildings, or other virtual assets that can be developed, traded, or used in gaming ecosystems.

The NFT Boom and Beyond

The NFT boom of 2021 brought digital art and collectibles into mainstream consciousness, with celebrities, athletes, and artists participating in this new economy. However, NFTs' value goes beyond just collectibles:

- *Intellectual property*: NFTs can represent intellectual property rights, offering new ways to manage, license, and monetize creative works.
- *Digital identity*: NFTs could be used to represent digital identities or personal credentials, providing secure and verifiable forms of identification.

The growth of NFTs signals a major shift in how people think about ownership in the digital age, with possibilities extending far beyond art and entertainment.

Central Bank Digital Currencies (CBDCs): The Future of Money?

As digital assets have gained popularity, governments and central banks have taken note. One of the most significant developments on the horizon is the emergence of **central bank digital currencies (CBDCs)**—digital versions of national currencies issued by central banks. While cryptocurrencies like Bitcoin operate independently of governments, CBDCs represent an effort by central authorities to harness the benefits of digital currencies while retaining control over monetary policy.

What Are CBDCs?

A **CBDC** is a digital version of a country's fiat currency, designed to be used as legal tender and issued by the central bank. Unlike cryptocurrencies, CBDCs are centrally controlled and backed by the government, offering the security and stability of traditional currencies with the efficiency and convenience of digital assets.

Why Are Governments Interested in CBDCs?

Governments are exploring CBDCs for several reasons:

- *Financial inclusion*: CBDCs could provide unbanked populations with access to digital financial services, helping close the gap in financial inclusion.
- *Efficiency*: Digital currencies can make payments faster, cheaper, and more secure, reducing reliance on physical cash.
- *Monetary policy*: Central banks can use CBDCs to enhance monetary policy tools, offering more precise control over money supply and inflation.

Countries like China, Sweden, and the Bahamas are already experimenting with CBDCs, and many others are in the research and development phase. While CBDCs promise to modernize financial systems, they also raise questions about privacy, surveillance, and the role of central banks in the digital economy.

The evolution of digital assets has been swift and transformative, moving from the early days of Bitcoin to the rise of DeFi, tokenization, NFTs, and the exploration of CBDCs. This evolution highlights the growing importance of digital assets in reshaping how we think about money, ownership, and value.

Chapter 6:
Why Invest in Digital Assets?

The rise of digital assets has fundamentally changed the landscape of investing, offering opportunities that traditional asset classes cannot match. As the world becomes increasingly digitized, investors are recognizing the potential for growth, diversification, and innovation that digital assets provide. In this chapter, we will explore the key reasons why investors should consider adding digital assets to their portfolios, examining the unique advantages they offer, as well as the risks and challenges that accompany them.

Diversification: Expanding Investment Horizons

One of the primary reasons to invest in digital assets is the opportunity for diversification. Just as traditional portfolios benefit from a mix of asset classes, adding digital assets can enhance diversification and potentially reduce overall risk.

Low Correlation with Traditional Assets

Digital assets, particularly cryptocurrencies, often have a low correlation with traditional asset classes such as stocks and bonds. This means that their price movements do not necessarily follow the same patterns as traditional investments:

- *Market Independence*: Digital assets can react differently to market events, economic shifts, or geopolitical crises. For instance, while traditional markets may decline during an economic downturn, cryptocurrencies may remain resilient or even thrive as investors seek alternative stores of value.
- *Global Reach*: Digital assets operate in a global, borderless environment, allowing for investment opportunities that are less influenced by local economic conditions.

By including digital assets in their portfolios, investors can reduce the overall volatility of their investments and potentially enhance returns over time.

High Growth Potential

The digital asset market is still in its early stages, and many assets have demonstrated remarkable growth potential. While past performance is not indicative of future results, the rapid appreciation of various cryptocurrencies and blockchain projects has captured the attention of investors worldwide.

Early Adoption Advantage

Investing in digital assets offers the opportunity to be part of a transformative movement. Early adopters of cryptocurrencies like Bitcoin and Ethereum have seen substantial returns:

- *Bitcoin*: Launched in 2009, Bitcoin's value has soared from mere cents to tens of thousands of dollars per coin, making it one of the best-performing assets of the past decade.
- *Ethereum*: As the foundation for numerous decentralized applications and DeFi projects, Ethereum has also experienced significant growth, driven by increased adoption and use cases.

Investors who enter the digital asset space at an early stage may benefit from similar growth trajectories as new projects and technologies emerge.

Innovation and Disruption

Digital assets are often at the forefront of innovation, challenging existing financial systems and creating new business models. By investing in this space, investors position themselves to benefit from disruptive technologies:

- *Decentralized Finance (DeFi)*: The growth of DeFi platforms offers opportunities for higher yields and alternative financial products that challenge traditional banking.

- *Tokenization*: The ability to tokenize real-world assets provides new avenues for investment and liquidity, expanding the range of assets available to investors.

Investors who embrace digital assets can tap into the potential of innovative technologies that are reshaping industries.

Accessibility and Inclusivity

Digital assets are more accessible than traditional financial markets, allowing a broader range of individuals to participate in investment opportunities. This democratization of finance is a compelling reason to consider investing in digital assets.

Lower Barriers to Entry

Investing in digital assets typically requires less capital than traditional assets:

- *Fractional Ownership*: Many cryptocurrencies can be purchased in fractional amounts, allowing investors to start with smaller investments. For example, investors can buy a fraction of a Bitcoin rather than needing to purchase an entire coin.
- *Global Access*: Digital assets can be bought and sold 24/7 through various online platforms, making

them accessible to anyone with an internet connection, regardless of geographic location.

This accessibility has the potential to empower individuals who may not have previously participated in traditional financial markets.

Financial Inclusion

Digital assets can play a vital role in promoting financial inclusion, particularly in underbanked regions:

- *Banking the Unbanked*: In many parts of the world, individuals lack access to traditional banking services. Digital assets provide an alternative means of saving, transacting, and investing without the need for a bank account.
- *Microfinance Opportunities*: Digital assets can facilitate microloans and peer-to-peer lending, enabling individuals to access capital and improve their financial situations.

By investing in digital assets, individuals can contribute to a more inclusive financial system that empowers others.

Hedge Against Inflation

In an environment of rising inflation and economic uncertainty, many investors seek assets that can preserve value over time. Digital assets, particularly cryptocurrencies, have emerged as potential hedges against inflation.

Deflationary Nature of Certain Cryptocurrencies

Cryptocurrencies like Bitcoin have a fixed supply, making them deflationary in nature:

- *Scarcity*: Bitcoin's supply is capped at 21 million coins, meaning that as demand increases, its value may rise due to its limited availability.
- *Alternative Store of Value*: Many investors view Bitcoin as a "digital gold" that can act as a store of value in times of economic uncertainty. As central banks continue to print money and stimulate economies, the appeal of cryptocurrencies as a hedge against inflation grows.

Investing in digital assets can provide a potential safeguard against the erosion of purchasing power.

Transparency and Security

The underlying technology of digital assets, blockchain, offers unique advantages in terms of transparency and security.

Immutable Records

Blockchain technology provides a transparent and immutable ledger of all transactions:

- *Transparency*: Every transaction is recorded on a public blockchain, allowing for verification and traceability. This level of transparency can enhance trust among participants and reduce fraud.
- *Security*: Blockchain's decentralized nature makes it inherently secure, as it is resistant to hacking and data manipulation. Assets held on a blockchain are protected by cryptographic techniques, ensuring that ownership and transaction history cannot be easily altered.

Investors can feel more confident knowing that their digital assets are secure and verifiable.

The Potential for Regulatory Clarity

As the digital asset market matures, regulatory frameworks are beginning to emerge. While regulatory uncertainty has been a concern for investors, increased clarity can enhance the legitimacy and stability of the market.

Evolving Regulations

Governments and regulatory bodies are increasingly recognizing the importance of digital assets:

- *Framework Development*: Many jurisdictions are working to establish regulations that govern the use, trading, and taxation of digital assets. These regulations can provide clarity for investors and foster a more stable investment environment.
- *Institutional Adoption*: As regulatory clarity improves, institutional investors are beginning to enter the digital asset space, bringing with them increased legitimacy and market confidence.

Investors who enter the market now may benefit from the potential upside as regulations solidify and mainstream acceptance grows.

Investing in digital assets offers a myriad of opportunities, from diversification and high growth potential to increased accessibility and protection against inflation. As the digital asset landscape continues to evolve, investors are encouraged to weigh the unique benefits against the associated risks.

While the digital asset market is not without its challenges—volatility, regulatory uncertainty, and security risks—those willing to embrace this new frontier may find themselves at the forefront of financial innovation and wealth creation. Understanding the reasons to invest in digital assets is crucial for anyone looking to navigate this transformative landscape and seize the opportunities it presents.

Chapter 6:
Who Should Invest in Digital Assets?

The digital asset landscape has rapidly evolved into a dynamic and promising investment arena, attracting a diverse array of participants. From seasoned investors and tech enthusiasts to newcomers eager to explore this burgeoning field, the question of who should invest in digital assets is increasingly relevant. This chapter delves into the profiles of individuals and organizations that may benefit from investing in digital assets, as well as considerations for potential investors to keep in mind before diving into this innovative market.

Tech-Savvy Investors

One of the primary groups drawn to digital assets is tech-savvy investors—those who are comfortable with technology and possess a basic understanding of how blockchain and cryptocurrencies work.

Early Adopters

Tech enthusiasts often seek out new technologies and innovations. Digital assets represent a frontier of innovation in finance and can offer unique investment opportunities:

- *Interest in Blockchain Technology*: Investors with an understanding of blockchain technology are better positioned to evaluate the potential of various digital assets. They can assess projects based on their technological merits and potential for adoption.
- *Willingness to Experiment*: Tech-savvy individuals are typically open to experimenting with new financial products and platforms. This willingness can lead to early investment in promising projects that

Ability to Navigate Complexity

Investing in digital assets often requires navigating complex platforms and understanding various terminologies (e.g., wallets, exchanges, smart contracts). Tech-savvy investors are usually equipped to handle these complexities, making them well-suited for participation in the digital asset market.

Risk-Tolerant Investors

Digital assets can be highly volatile and speculative. As such, investors with a high tolerance for risk may find the potential rewards of investing in digital assets appealing.

High-Reward Potential

While digital assets can experience significant price fluctuations, they also offer the potential for substantial gains:

- *Historical Performance*: Some cryptocurrencies have experienced astronomical price increases over relatively short periods. Early investors in Bitcoin and Ethereum, for example, have realized extraordinary returns.
- *Diversification Opportunity*: Risk-tolerant investors often seek to diversify their portfolios with assets that have high growth potential, and digital assets can provide that opportunity.

Long-Term Perspective

Investors willing to accept short-term volatility in exchange for long-term gains are better suited for digital asset investments. Holding digital assets over extended periods can help mitigate the effects of market fluctuations.

Institutional Investors

In recent years, institutional investors have begun to enter the digital asset market, recognizing the potential for portfolio diversification and the growth of new investment products.

Diversification and Portfolio Allocation

Institutional investors, such as pension funds, hedge funds, and asset managers, are increasingly viewing digital assets as a viable asset class for diversification:

- *Strategic Allocation*: Institutions may allocate a small percentage of their portfolios to digital assets, using them as a hedge against inflation and economic uncertainty.
- *Emerging Investment Products*: The development of financial products like exchange-traded funds (ETFs) and regulated futures contracts has made it easier for institutions to gain exposure to digital assets.

Competitive Edge

As competition for yield and returns intensifies, institutional investors are exploring digital assets to gain a competitive edge in the evolving financial landscape. This trend may lead to further mainstream acceptance of digital assets.

Younger Generations and Millennials

Younger generations, particularly millennials and Gen Z, are driving much of the demand for digital assets. Many of these individuals have grown up with technology and are more open to alternative investment vehicles.

Comfort with Digital Technologies

Younger investors are often more comfortable using digital platforms for trading and investing. They are likely to embrace digital assets as part of their investment strategies:

- *Digital Natives*: Being raised in the digital age, younger generations tend to have a better understanding of online transactions and digital currencies.
- *Interest in New Investment Trends*: Millennials and Gen Z are often attracted to new trends, including DeFi, NFTs, and cryptocurrency projects, making them eager participants in the digital asset space.

Investment for the Future

Younger investors often prioritize long-term growth and are willing to invest in innovative technologies that can shape the future of finance. Digital assets align with their forward-thinking approach.

Socially Conscious Investors

As awareness of social and environmental issues grows, socially conscious investors are seeking investments that align with their values. Digital assets can provide unique opportunities in this regard.

Decentralization and Empowerment

Digital assets often promote decentralization and inclusivity, aligning with the values of socially conscious investors:

- *Financial Inclusion*: Digital assets have the potential to provide financial services to the unbanked and underbanked populations worldwide, empowering individuals in developing regions.
- *Supporting Innovative Projects*: Many blockchain projects focus on social impact, sustainability, and transparency, making them appealing to investors who prioritize ethical considerations.

Investment in Positive Change

Socially conscious investors can find opportunities to support projects that create positive change in the world while also generating financial returns.

Individuals Seeking Alternative Investments

Investors looking to diversify their portfolios beyond traditional assets like stocks and bonds may find digital assets to be an attractive alternative.

Inflation Hedge

With rising inflation concerns, many investors are seeking assets that can help preserve purchasing power:

- *Digital Gold*: Cryptocurrencies like Bitcoin are increasingly viewed as a hedge against inflation, similar to gold, providing an alternative store of value.
- *Diversification Benefits*: Digital assets can serve as a means of diversification that helps mitigate risks associated with traditional asset classes.

Access to New Markets

Investing in digital assets opens the door to new markets and opportunities that were previously unavailable to individual investors. This expanded access can enhance overall portfolio performance.

Digital assets present a compelling investment opportunity for a diverse range of individuals and organizations. Tech-savvy investors, risk-tolerant individuals, institutional investors, younger generations, socially conscious investors, and those seeking alternative investments can all find value in this dynamic space.

However, potential investors should carefully consider their risk tolerance, investment goals, and the complexities of the digital asset market before diving in.

Chapter 7:
A New Paradigm of Ownership

The emergence of digital assets has fundamentally transformed our understanding of ownership, introducing a new paradigm that challenges traditional notions of property, value, and trust. As we delve into this chapter, we will explore how digital assets, particularly cryptocurrencies and blockchain technology, are redefining ownership in the modern world. This exploration will encompass the implications for individuals, businesses, and society as a whole.

The Concept of Ownership

Traditionally, ownership has been associated with tangible assets—land, buildings, vehicles, and physical goods. Ownership implies control, responsibility, and the ability to transfer or sell the asset at will. However, in the digital age, ownership is evolving, giving rise to new forms of assets that are not confined to physical manifestations.

Digital Assets Defined

Digital assets refer to any asset that exists in a digital format and is owned by an individual or entity. This category includes cryptocurrencies, digital art (NFTs), virtual real estate, and tokenized representations of real-world assets. Each of these assets presents unique characteristics that challenge conventional ownership principles:

- *Intangibility*: Digital assets are often intangible, existing solely in digital form without a physical counterpart. This raises questions about how we conceptualize and validate ownership.
- *Transferability*: The ability to transfer digital assets instantaneously across borders introduces new complexities regarding the nature of ownership and the rights associated with it.

Blockchain Technology: The Backbone of Digital Ownership

At the heart of the new paradigm of ownership lies blockchain technology, which provides the infrastructure for creating, storing, and transferring digital assets.

Decentralization and Transparency

Blockchain technology operates on a decentralized network, allowing for transparent and immutable records of ownership:

- *Immutable Ownership Records*: Each transaction recorded on a blockchain is permanent and cannot be altered, ensuring a reliable history of ownership. This feature eliminates the need for centralized

authorities to verify ownership, as the blockchain serves as a trusted ledger.
- *Greater Trust*: The transparency of blockchain enhances trust among parties involved in transactions, as anyone can verify ownership and transaction history without relying on intermediaries.

Smart Contracts and Automated Ownership Transfers

Smart contracts—self-executing contracts with the terms of the agreement directly written into code—further transform ownership dynamics:

- *Automatic Execution*: Smart contracts facilitate automated transfers of ownership based on predefined conditions, reducing the need for intermediaries and streamlining transactions.
- *Programmable Ownership*: Ownership can be programmed to include specific conditions, such as royalties for creators on subsequent sales of digital art. This feature introduces a new layer of control and benefit for asset creators.

Tokenization: Redefining Value and Ownership

Tokenization is a process that converts real-world assets into digital tokens on a blockchain, allowing for fractional ownership and increased liquidity.

Fractional Ownership

Tokenization enables individuals to own fractions of high-value assets, such as real estate, art, or collectibles:

- *Accessibility*: This democratizes access to investment opportunities that were previously available only to affluent individuals. By lowering the barriers to entry, tokenization allows a broader range of investors to participate in asset ownership.
- *Liquidity*: Fractional ownership also enhances liquidity, as tokens can be traded on digital asset exchanges, enabling investors to buy and sell their shares more easily.

New Valuation Models

Tokenization introduces new methods of valuing assets that consider their digital counterparts. This shift in valuation can lead to innovative investment strategies and opportunities for diversification.

Non-Fungible Tokens (NFTs): The Future of Digital Ownership

Non-fungible tokens (NFTs) have garnered significant attention as unique digital assets representing ownership of specific items or content, ranging from digital art and music to virtual real estate and in-game items.

Unique Provenance and Authenticity

NFTs provide a mechanism for verifying the uniqueness and provenance of digital assets:

- *Proof of Ownership*: Each NFT contains metadata that verifies its authenticity, allowing creators and collectors to establish ownership and provenance easily.
- *Cultural Value*: The ability to prove ownership of unique digital assets creates new avenues for cultural and artistic expression, as artists can monetize their work directly and maintain control over their intellectual property.

Shifting Cultural Norms

The rise of NFTs is reshaping cultural norms around ownership and value:

- *Digital Collectibles*: NFTs challenge the traditional concept of collectibles by allowing for digital versions that can be traded, displayed, and appreciated in online environments.
- *Community and Membership*: Some NFTs grant access to exclusive communities or experiences, redefining ownership as a means of belonging and participation rather than mere possession.

Implications for Businesses and Society

The new paradigm of ownership brought about by digital assets has far-reaching implications for businesses and society as a whole.

Business Models and Innovation

Organizations are adapting to the changing landscape by exploring new business models based on digital assets:

- *Token-Based Economies*: Businesses can create their own tokens to incentivize customer engagement, loyalty, and participation in their ecosystems.
- *Crowdfunding and Investment Opportunities*: Blockchain enables new forms of fundraising, allowing startups to issue tokens representing equity or utility to raise capital directly from investors.

Legal and Regulatory Challenges

As ownership definitions evolve, legal and regulatory frameworks must adapt to address the complexities of digital asset ownership:

- *Intellectual Property Rights*: Determining ownership rights for digital assets, particularly NFTs, raises questions about copyright, royalties, and creator rights.

- *Consumer Protection*: Ensuring consumer protection in the rapidly evolving digital asset space is essential to foster trust and participation.

The Future of Ownership

As digital assets continue to gain traction, the concept of ownership will likely continue to evolve. The new paradigm is characterized by flexibility, innovation, and inclusivity, as individuals and organizations explore the potential of digital assets.

A. A Shift in Mindset

The emergence of digital assets encourages a shift in mindset regarding ownership:

- *Fluidity of Ownership*: Digital ownership is becoming more fluid, with assets able to change hands quickly and easily across digital platforms.
- *Collaboration and Sharing*: New models of ownership emphasize collaboration and sharing, allowing for communal ownership and access rather than traditional individual possession.

Embracing Change

As society adapts to the realities of digital ownership, embracing change and innovation will be crucial for individuals and businesses alike. The ability to navigate this new paradigm will determine success in a rapidly changing digital economy.

The rise of digital assets heralds a new paradigm of ownership that challenges traditional notions and opens up new possibilities for individuals and businesses. Through blockchain technology, tokenization, and NFTs, we are witnessing a transformation in how we define, establish, and transfer ownership.

As we navigate this evolving landscape, understanding the implications and opportunities presented by digital assets will be essential for embracing the future of ownership. The journey toward a more inclusive, transparent, and innovative approach to ownership is just beginning, and those who adapt to these changes will be at the forefront of this new era in finance and value creation.

Chapter 8:
Preparing for the Journey

Embarking on the journey of investing in digital assets is akin to setting sail into uncharted waters. The landscape is dynamic, filled with opportunities and challenges that require careful navigation. In this chapter, we will outline the essential steps to prepare for this journey, ensuring that both novice and experienced investors are well-equipped to make informed decisions in the digital asset space.

Educate Yourself: Building a Strong Foundation

Before diving into the world of digital assets, it is crucial to build a solid foundation of knowledge.

Understand the Basics

Start by familiarizing yourself with the fundamental concepts of digital assets:

- *Cryptocurrencies*: Learn about the different types of cryptocurrencies, their underlying technologies, and how they function. Understanding Bitcoin, Ethereum, and altcoins is essential for making informed investment decisions.

- *Blockchain Technology*: Explore the technology that powers digital assets. Understanding blockchain's decentralization, immutability, and security features will give you insight into how digital assets operate.

Stay Informed About Industry Trends

The digital asset space is rapidly evolving. Stay informed by following industry news, participating in online forums, and engaging with reputable resources:

- *News Platforms*: Subscribe to cryptocurrency news websites, podcasts, and newsletters that provide timely updates and analyses.
- *Community Engagement*: Join online communities and forums, such as Reddit and Discord, where you can learn from others, share experiences, and gain insights from industry experts.

Set Clear Investment Goals

Before making any investments, define your objectives. Understanding your goals will help you formulate a strategy tailored to your financial situation and risk tolerance.

Identify Your Investment Horizon

Determine whether you are looking for short-term gains or long-term wealth accumulation:

- *Short-Term vs. Long-Term*: If you aim for quick returns, you may engage in active trading. If your focus is on long-term growth, you might consider holding digital assets for an extended period.
- *Market Conditions*: Be aware of market trends and conditions that may influence your investment horizon.

Define Your Risk Tolerance

Assess your risk appetite to determine how much of your portfolio you are willing to allocate to digital assets:

- *Risk Assessment*: Consider factors such as your age, financial situation, and investment experience when assessing your risk tolerance.
- *Diversification*: To manage risk effectively, diversify your investments across different asset classes, including traditional assets and digital assets.

Choose the Right Digital Assets

With a foundational understanding and clear investment goals, the next step is to select the digital assets that align with your strategy.

Research Different Types of Digital Assets

Explore various categories of digital assets to identify which ones resonate with your investment philosophy:

- *Cryptocurrencies*: Investigate major cryptocurrencies like Bitcoin and Ethereum, as well as promising altcoins with strong fundamentals.
- *Non-Fungible Tokens (NFTs)*: Consider investing in NFTs representing art, music, virtual real estate, or collectibles. Research the projects behind the NFTs to evaluate their potential value.
- *DeFi Projects*: Explore decentralized finance (DeFi) platforms that offer lending, borrowing, and yield farming opportunities.

Evaluate Projects and Teams

Conduct thorough research on the projects and teams behind the digital assets you are considering:

- *Whitepapers and Roadmaps*: Review project whitepapers and roadmaps to understand their goals, technology, and development plans.
- *Team Experience*: Investigate the backgrounds and experience of the teams behind the projects. A strong team with a proven track record increases the likelihood of success.

Select a Secure and Reliable Wallet

A critical aspect of investing in digital assets is choosing the right wallet to store your assets securely.

Understand Different Wallet Types

Digital wallets come in various forms, each with its own features and security levels:

- *Hot Wallets*: These are online wallets that are convenient for trading and quick access but are more susceptible to hacking. Use them for day-to-day transactions.
- *Cold Wallets*: Cold wallets, such as hardware wallets, store your assets offline, providing enhanced security. They are ideal for long-term storage.

Implement Strong Security Practices

To protect your digital assets, adopt robust security measures:

- *Two-Factor Authentication (2FA)*: Enable 2FA on your wallet and exchange accounts for an extra layer of security.
- *Backup Your Wallet*: Regularly back up your wallet and keep your recovery phrases secure. This practice ensures you can access your assets even if you lose your device.

Stay Compliant with Regulations

As the digital asset landscape matures, regulatory frameworks are evolving. Familiarize yourself with the regulations that govern digital asset investments in your jurisdiction.

Tax Considerations

Understand the tax implications of buying, selling, and trading digital assets:

- *Tax Reporting*: Keep accurate records of your transactions, as many jurisdictions require reporting capital gains on cryptocurrency investments.
- *Consult a Professional*: If needed, consult a tax professional with expertise in digital asset taxation to ensure compliance.

Legal Compliance

Stay informed about the legal framework surrounding digital assets, including securities regulations and anti-money laundering (AML) requirements. Adhering to these regulations is crucial for protecting yourself as an investor.

Develop an Investment Strategy

With knowledge, goals, and a secure setup in place, create a personalized investment strategy to guide your decisions.

Asset Allocation

Decide how much of your overall portfolio you will allocate to digital assets:

- *Diversification Strategy*: Aim to strike a balance between risk and reward by diversifying across different types of digital assets and traditional investments.
- *Rebalancing*: Regularly review your portfolio and rebalance as needed to maintain your desired asset allocation.

Stay Disciplined

Emotional decision-making can lead to impulsive actions. Cultivate discipline in your investment strategy:

- *Set Entry and Exit Points*: Establish predetermined entry and exit points for your investments based on research and analysis.
- *Avoid FOMO*: Resist the urge to chase trends or panic sell during market downturns. Stick to your strategy and remain focused on your long-term goals.

Embrace Continuous Learning

The digital asset landscape is ever-changing. To thrive, commit to ongoing learning and adaptation.

Follow Industry Developments

Stay updated on emerging technologies, market trends, and regulatory changes that may impact your investments:

- *Webinars and Conferences*: Participate in webinars, conferences, and workshops to gain insights from industry experts and network with fellow investors.
- *Adapt to New Information*: Be open to adjusting your investment strategy based on new information and evolving market conditions.

Learn from Experiences

Reflect on your investment experiences, both successes and failures, to improve your decision-making:

- *Keep a Journal*: Document your investment journey, including your strategies, outcomes, and lessons learned. This practice can help you refine your approach over time.

Preparing for the journey of digital assets requires careful consideration, education, and planning. By building a strong foundation of knowledge, setting clear investment goals, and developing a disciplined strategy, investors can navigate the dynamic landscape of digital assets with confidence.

As the digital asset ecosystem continues to evolve, adaptability and a commitment to continuous learning will be essential for seizing the opportunities that lie ahead. With the right preparation, investors can embark on this journey and harness the transformative potential of digital assets to achieve their financial objectives.

Chapter 9:
Welcome to the future of investing

As we conclude this exploration of digital assets, it is essential to recognize the transformative journey you are about to embark upon as a new investor. The landscape of finance is evolving at an unprecedented pace, driven by technological advancements and the growing acceptance of digital currencies and assets. This new era presents a wealth of opportunities, challenges, and responsibilities that you will encounter as you navigate the world of digital investments. In this concluding chapter, we will delve into the significance of this journey, the mindset you should cultivate, the resources at your disposal, and the long-term vision you should adopt as you step into the realm of digital assets.

The Significance of Digital Assets

Digital assets have fundamentally changed the way we view ownership, investment, and wealth creation. They represent not just a new asset class, but also a shift in the financial paradigm that embraces decentralization, transparency, and democratization. By investing in digital assets, you are participating in a movement that is redefining how value is exchanged and stored across the globe.

A New Era of Financial Inclusion

One of the most compelling aspects of digital assets is their potential to promote financial inclusion. For many individuals worldwide, traditional financial systems have been inaccessible, leaving them without avenues for investment and wealth creation. Digital assets provide an opportunity for anyone with internet access to participate in the financial markets, breaking down barriers and empowering a new generation of investors.

Embracing Innovation

Investing in digital assets places you at the forefront of financial innovation. The rapid development of blockchain technology, decentralized finance (DeFi), and non-fungible tokens (NFTs) is reshaping industries beyond finance, including art, real estate, and gaming. As a new investor, you have the chance to explore and engage with these innovative solutions, potentially benefiting from their growth and success.

Cultivating the Right Mindset

Your mindset will be a critical determinant of your success in the digital asset space. It is essential to approach this journey with an open and adaptable mindset that embraces learning, resilience, and growth.

Embrace a Growth Mindset

A growth mindset enables you to view challenges as opportunities for learning and improvement. In the world of digital assets, you will encounter volatility, uncertainty, and rapid changes. By embracing a growth mindset, you can learn from both successes and failures, adapt your strategies, and continuously refine your approach to investing.

Manage Your Emotions

The emotional aspect of investing cannot be overstated. The thrill of market highs and the anxiety of market lows can cloud judgment and lead to impulsive decisions. Cultivating emotional intelligence will help you remain level-headed during turbulent times. Develop strategies to manage your emotions, such as setting predetermined investment goals, maintaining a diversified portfolio, and practicing mindfulness techniques.

Leveraging Resources for Success

The journey of investing in digital assets is one that requires continuous learning and adaptation. Fortunately, a wealth of resources is available to help you navigate this complex landscape.

Educational Resources

Invest in your education by exploring a variety of resources tailored to your learning style:

- *Online Courses*: Platforms like Coursera, Udemy, and Khan Academy offer courses on blockchain technology, cryptocurrency investing, and digital asset management. Choose courses that align with your current knowledge and skill level.
- *Books and Articles*: Read books, articles, and whitepapers authored by industry experts to deepen your understanding of digital assets and the technology behind them.
- *Podcasts and Webinars*: Listen to podcasts and attend webinars to gain insights from thought leaders and practitioners in the digital asset space.

Community Engagement

Engaging with the broader community of digital asset investors can provide valuable support, insights, and networking opportunities:

- *Online Forums*: Join platforms such as Reddit, Discord, and specialized crypto forums where you can ask questions, share experiences, and learn from others in the community.
- *Local Meetups*: Seek out local meetups or events in your area where you can connect with fellow investors, attend presentations, and participate in discussions about digital assets.

Developing a Long-Term Vision

As you begin your investment journey, it is vital to develop a long-term vision that guides your decisions and actions. Digital assets may experience significant price fluctuations, but maintaining a long-term perspective can help you stay focused on your financial goals.

Establish Your Financial Goals

Define your investment goals and timelines, keeping in mind your risk tolerance, financial situation, and personal aspirations:

- *Short-Term vs. Long-Term Goals*: Identify whether your goals are short-term (e.g., quick gains) or long-term (e.g., retirement savings). Understanding your objectives will inform your investment strategy.
- *Portfolio Allocation*: Consider how much of your portfolio you wish to allocate to digital assets versus traditional investments. A well-balanced portfolio can help mitigate risk and enhance returns.

Stay Committed to Your Vision

The digital asset landscape is marked by volatility and uncertainty. To succeed, it is crucial to remain committed to your long-term vision and avoid making hasty decisions based on short-term market fluctuations. Periodically review your investment strategy and adjust as needed, but remain focused on your overarching goals.

The Importance of Responsible Investing

As you embark on your journey into the world of digital assets, it is vital to prioritize responsible investing practices. The potential for high returns often comes with inherent risks, and it is essential to approach your investments with caution and integrity.

Conduct Thorough Research

Before investing in any digital asset, conduct thorough due diligence to understand the project, its team, technology, and market potential. Be wary of hype and speculation, and focus on the fundamentals that drive value.

Be Wary of Scams

The digital asset space has attracted its share of scams and fraudulent schemes. Protect yourself by being cautious and skeptical of offers that seem too good to be true. Always use reputable exchanges, wallets, and platforms, and verify the legitimacy of projects before investing.

A Bright Future Awaits

As we welcome you to the world of digital assets, we invite you to embrace the possibilities that lie ahead. This is an exciting and transformative journey filled with potential for growth, innovation, and financial empowerment.

Your Role in Shaping the Future

By participating in the digital asset ecosystem, you are not just an investor; you are a part of a broader movement that is shaping the future of finance and commerce. Your decisions, actions, and engagement will contribute to the evolution of this space and influence how digital assets are perceived and integrated into our daily lives.

Celebrate Your Journey

As you take your first steps into the realm of digital assets, celebrate the journey ahead. Each milestone, whether big or small, represents progress and learning. Your commitment to continuous education, community engagement, and responsible investing will pave the way for success.

The world of digital assets is a dynamic and ever-changing landscape that offers immense opportunities for those willing to explore its depths. Welcome aboard this exciting journey. As you navigate the waters of digital investment, may you find growth, fulfillment, and a renewed sense of financial empowerment. The future of investing is digital, and it is yours to shape.

Welcome to the digital frontier!

www.ingramcontent.com/pod-product-compliance
Lightning Source LLC
Chambersburg PA
CBHW071101240526
45471CB00016B/2299